J 941 V217u
Van, R. L.,
United Kingdom /

UNITED KINGDOM

R.L. Van

Big Buddy Books
An Imprint of Abdo Publishing
abdobooks.com

abdobooks.com

Published by Abdo Publishing, a division of ABDO, PO Box 398166, Minneapolis, Minnesota 55439. Copyright © 2023 by Abdo Consulting Group, Inc. International copyrights reserved in all countries. No part of this book may be reproduced in any form without written permission from the publisher. Big Buddy Books™ is a trademark and logo of Abdo Publishing.

Printed in the United States of America, North Mankato, Minnesota
102022
012023

Design: Emily O'Malley, Mighty Media, Inc.
Production: Mighty Media, Inc.
Editor: Jessica Rusick
Cover Photograph: alberto cervantes/Shutterstock Images
Interior Photographs: Aarti K Singh/Shutterstock Images, p. 19; Cubankite/Shutterstock Images, p. 23; Electric Egg/Shutterstock Images, p. 27 (bottom); elxeneize/Shutterstock Images, p. 27 (top left); Everett Collection/Shutterstock Images, pp. 11, 28 (bottom); Frank Augstein/AP Images, p. 29 (top right); hilderifi/Shutterstock Images, p. 7 (map); Kanuman/Shutterstock Images, p. 25; Kiev.Victor/Shutterstock Images, p. 6 (bottom); lazyllama/Shutterstock Images, p. 13; Library of Congress, p. 29 (top left); lukulo/iStockphoto, pp. 5 (compass), 7 (compass); mark reinstein/Shutterstock Images, p. 29 (bottom); Michal 11/Shutterstock Images, p. 28 (top); Mr Nai/Shutterstock Images, p. 26 (left); Nature's Charm/Shutterstock Images, p. 26 (right); 1000 Words/Shutterstock Images, p. 17; Pigprox/Shutterstock Images, p. 30 (currency); Pyty/Shutterstock Images, p. 5 (map); r.classen/Shutterstock Images, p. 6 (top); S-F/Shutterstock Images, p. 27 (top right); salarko/Shutterstock Images, p. 15; Tinseltown/Shutterstock Images, p. 21; VectorShop/Shutterstock Images, p. 30 (flag); Wang Sing/Shutterstock Images, p. 9; zaeball/Shutterstock Images, p. 6 (middle)
Design Elements: Mighty Media, Inc.
Country population and area figures taken from the CIA World Factbook

Library of Congress Control Number: 2022940517

Publisher's Cataloging-in-Publication Data
Names: Van, R.L., author.
Title: United Kingdom / by R.L. Van
Description: Minneapolis, Minnesota : Abdo Publishing, 2023 | Series: Countries | Includes online resources and index.
Identifiers: ISBN 9781532199769 (lib. bdg.) | ISBN 9781098274962 (ebook)
Subjects: LCSH: United Kingdom--Juvenile literature. | Europe--Juvenile literature. | Great Britain--History--Juvenile literature. | Geography--Juvenile literature.
Classification: DDC 941--dc23

CONTENTS

Passport to the United Kingdom 4
Important Cities 6
The United Kingdom in History 8
An Important Symbol 12
Across the Land 14
Earning a Living 16
Life in the United Kingdom 18
Famous Faces 20
A Great Country 24
Tour Book 26
Timeline 28
The United Kingdom Up Close 30
Glossary 31
Online Resources 31
Index 32

1

PASSPORT TO THE UNITED KINGDOM

The **United** Kingdom (UK) is a country in western Europe. It includes England, Scotland, Wales, and Northern Ireland. More than 67 million people live there.

2

IMPORTANT CITIES

London is the UK's **capital** and largest **metropolitan area**. It is known for its history and culture.

Manchester is the UK's second-largest metropolitan area. It is known for its sports and scientific discoveries.

Birmingham is the UK's third-largest metropolitan area. It is a center of manufacturing and tourism.

SAY IT

London
LUHN-den

Manchester
MAN-chess-tuhr

Birmingham
BUHR-ming-ham

DID YOU KNOW?

London was founded in the year 43.

3

THE UNITED KINGDOM IN HISTORY

People have lived in the **United Kingdom** for thousands of years. Different groups settled the land. In 1536, England and Wales united. In 1707, Scotland joined them. Together, these countries formed the Kingdom of **Great Britain**.

Queen Anne was the first ruler of the Kingdom of Great Britain.

In 1801, **Great Britain** joined with Ireland to form the **United** Kingdom. By 1900, the UK ruled many parts of the world. Over the years, many of these places became independent. Because of this and the costs of **World War II**, the UK had lost much of its **empire** by 2000. But the country remained strong.

The UK struggled during World War II. Many of its cities were destroyed.

4

AN IMPORTANT SYMBOL

The **United** Kingdom's flag was adopted in 1801. The crosses stand for England, Scotland, and Ireland.

The UK is a **parliamentary constitutional monarchy**. Parliament makes laws. The king or queen is head of state. The prime minister is head of government.

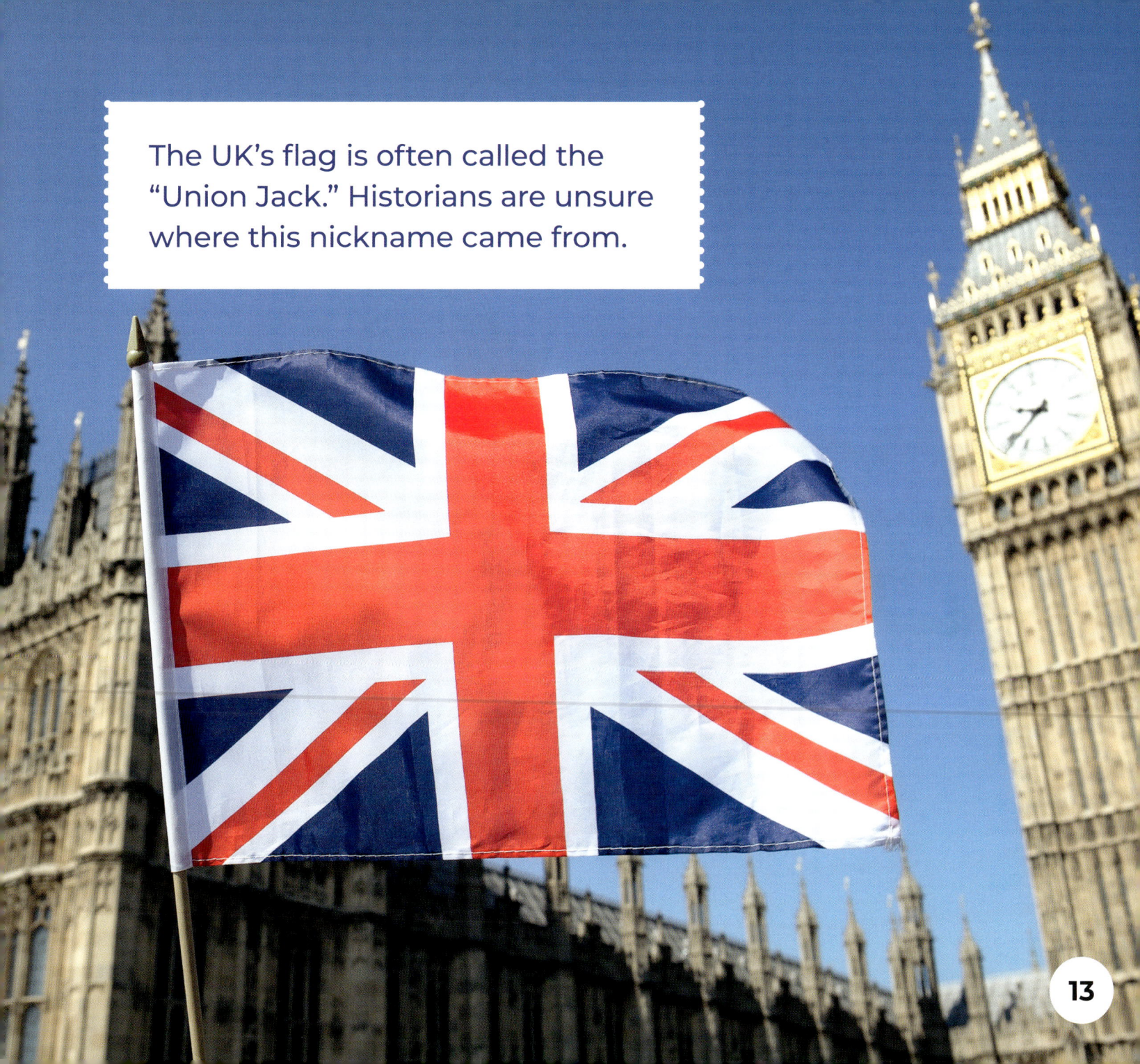

The UK's flag is often called the "Union Jack." Historians are unsure where this nickname came from.

5

ACROSS THE LAND

The **United** Kingdom has valleys, **moors**, and mountains. The Thames and Severn are the longest rivers.

Deer, badgers, stoats, and rabbits live in the UK. There are many types of birds. Bluebells, peat moss, and oak trees grow there.

SAY IT

Thames
TEHMZ

Bluebells bloom in spring. The flowers grow close together and smell sweet.

EARNING A LIVING

Factory workers in the UK make cars, airplane parts, and medicines. Most people have service jobs, such as nursing or teaching.

The UK's **natural resources** include oil, natural gas, coal, and fish. Farmers produce grains, apples, potatoes, and animal products.

Many Mini Cooper cars are built in Oxford, England.

7

LIFE IN THE UNITED KINGDOM

Popular foods in the UK include fish and chips and Yorkshire pudding. People often drink tea.

Soccer, cricket, and rugby are favorite sports in the UK. Many people belong to the Church of England.

Yorkshire puddings are similar to popovers. They are sometimes filled with meat and gravy.

8

FAMOUS FACES

Tom Holland was born near London, England. He began acting when he was 12 years old. Holland is known for playing the superhero Spider-Man in Marvel movies. He also played Nathan Drake in the movie *Uncharted*.

Tom Holland is a trained dancer and gymnast. He often does his own movie stunts!

Ed Sheeran was born in Halifax, England. He learned to play the guitar when he was 11 years old. Sheeran became famous when his song "The A Team" was released in 2011. Over the years, he put out many successful albums. By 2022, he had won four Grammy Awards.

Ed Sheeran is one of the best-selling music artists of all time.

9

A GREAT COUNTRY

The **United** Kingdom has beautiful land and a rich history and culture. The people and places of the United Kingdom help make the world a more interesting place.

The Scottish Highlands are home to the UK's highest mountains.

TOUR BOOK

If you ever visit the United Kingdom, here are some places to go and things to do!

SEE

Visit Stonehenge in southern England. No one knows why this ancient stone circle was built.

SIP

Stop for a themed children's afternoon tea in London. You can even have your tea on a bus tour!

SWIM

Check out the Fairy Pools on the Isle of Skye in Scotland. Even though they are cold, many people swim in them!

EXPLORE

Visit Giant's Causeway in Northern Ireland. The unusual rock shapes formed from lava flows.

EAT

Go to Cadbury World in Birmingham to learn about the history of chocolate.

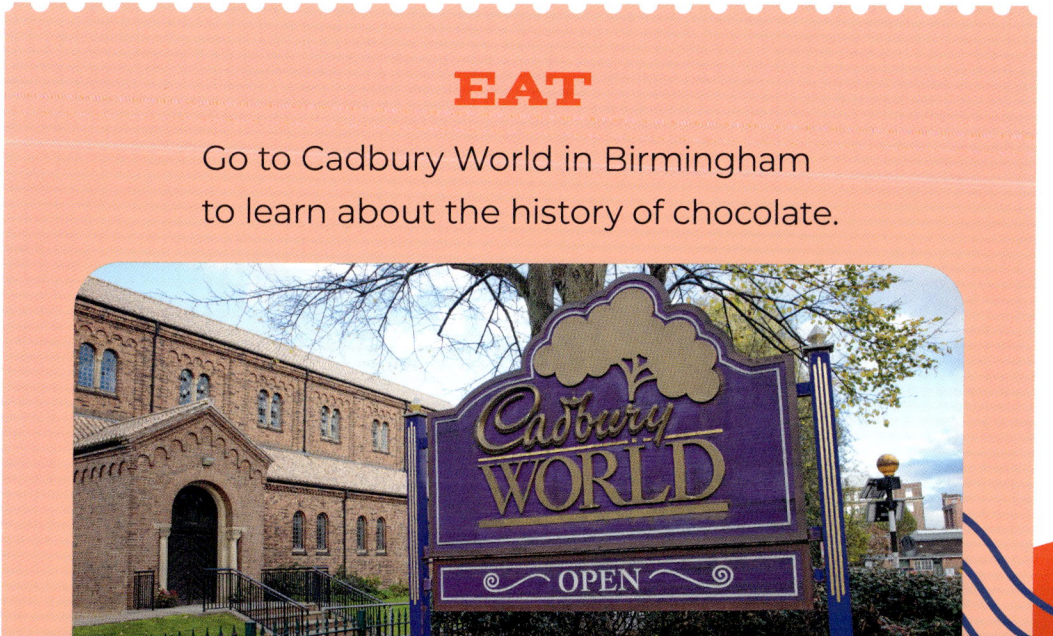

TIMELINE

ABOUT 1000 BCE
People began living on Castle Rock in present-day Scotland. Edinburgh Castle was built here.

1558 CE
Elizabeth I became the queen of England. Her rule is considered the Golden Age of England.

1801
Ireland and **Great Britain** joined, forming the **United** Kingdom.

1962

The Beatles recorded their first song. The rock band from Liverpool, England, became world-famous.

2022

Queen Elizabeth II died on September 8. She had been queen for 70 years and is the longest-serving ruler in UK history.

1979

Margaret Thatcher became the UK's first female prime minister.

2016

Voters elected to leave the **European Union**. This became known as "Brexit."

THE UNITED KINGDOM UP CLOSE

Official Name
United Kingdom of Great Britain and Northern Ireland

Flag

Population
67,791,400 (2022 est.)
22nd-most-populated country

Total Area
94,058 square miles
(243,610 sq km)
78th-largest country

Official Languages
English, Scots Gaelic (Scotland), Welsh (Wales)

Capital
London

Currency
British pound

Form of Government
Parliamentary constitutional monarchy

National Anthem
"God Save the Queen" or "God Save the King"

GLOSSARY

capital—a city where government leaders meet.

empire—a large group of states or countries under one ruler called an emperor or empress.

European Union—an organization bringing together countries mostly in Europe under certain government and economic policies.

Great Britain—the island consisting of England, Scotland, and Wales.

metropolitan area—a large city and its surrounding cities and suburbs.

moor—open land with poor farming soil.

natural resources—useful and valuable supplies from nature.

parliamentary constitutional monarchy—a form of government in which a parliament makes laws and a king or queen has only those powers given by a country's laws and constitution.

united—joined together for purpose or action.

World War II—a war fought in Europe, Asia, and Africa from 1939 to 1945.

ONLINE RESOURCES

To learn more about the United Kingdom, please visit **abdobooklinks.com** or scan this QR code. These links are routinely monitored and updated to provide the most current information available.

INDEX

animals, 14, 16

Beatles, 29
Birmingham, 6, 7, 27
businesses, 6, 16, 17

Cadbury World, 27

Edinburgh Castle, 28
England, 4, 7, 8, 12, 17, 18, 20, 22, 26, 28, 29
Europe, 4, 29

Fairy Pools, 27
flag, 12, 13, 30
food, 6, 16, 18, 19, 27

Giant's Causeway, 27
government, 8, 9, 10, 12, 28, 29, 30
Great Britain, 8, 9, 10, 28, 30

Highlands, 25
Holland, Tom, 20, 21

Ireland, 5, 10, 12, 28

language, 30
London, 6, 7, 20, 26, 30

Manchester, 6, 7

natural resources, 16
Northern Ireland, 4, 7, 27, 30

plants, 14, 15, 16
population, 4, 7, 30

religion, 18
rivers, 14
royalty, 9, 12, 28, 29, 30

Scotland, 4, 7, 8, 12, 25, 27, 28, 30
Sheeran, Ed, 22, 23
size, 30
sports, 18
Stonehenge, 26

Thatcher, Margaret, 29

Wales, 4, 7, 8, 30
World War II, 10, 11